One Giant Leap

by Sharon Franklin

Scott Foresman
is an imprint of

Glenview, Illinois • Boston, Massachusetts • Chandler, Arizona
Upper Saddle River, New Jersey

ISBN 13: 978-0-328-51956-9
ISBN 10:   0-328-51956-1

4 5 6 7 8 9 10 V0FL 14 13 12 11

July 16, 1969

The Apollo 11 crew

"12 . . . 11 . . . 10 . . . 9 . . . Ignition sequence starts." People hold their breath as a huge ball of flame appears at the base of the Saturn V booster rocket. The Saturn V will propel the Apollo 11 **astronauts** into space. It is so tall that the astronauts had to use an elevator to get to the spacecraft at the top of the rocket.

"6 . . . 5 . . ." Steam from the launch site billows up, producing huge clouds that cover the area around the launch pad. People watching grow strangely quiet. No one says a word.

"4 . . . 3 . . ." The shudder from the launch pad is felt miles from the Kennedy Space Center in Florida. The two million people who crowd the nearby grandstands, roads, and beaches to see the launch feel it. A different kind of shudder is felt by the astronauts' families and everyone at Mission Control in Houston, where the space shuttle flight is monitored. Millions of people around the world watch and listen.

3

No one feels the excitement more than the three astronauts on board Apollo 11. The day is finally here for Neil A. Armstrong, Michael Collins, and Edwin E. "Buzz" Aldrin, Jr. It is the morning of July 16, 1969. They have prepared carefully and are on their way to the moon.

"2 . . . 1 . . . 0 . . . All engines running. Liftoff! We have a liftoff, thirty-two minutes past the hour. Liftoff on Apollo 11 . . . Tower cleared!"

People on the ground cheer, clap, cry, hug, and scream with joy—responses echo around the world. The Saturn V slowly moves into its correct flight path.

Over the next eight days, the astronauts of the Apollo 11 space **capsule** will land a craft on the moon, go out to walk on the **lunar** surface, and then return to Earth. Some people called it the biggest single step in human history.

People watching on the beach shield their eyes and strain to see the spacecraft in the sky until it disappears. They pack up their blankets and picnic baskets and prepare to leave. But inside the command **module** of Apollo 11, the hard work is just beginning.

Less than three minutes after liftoff, the first stage of the Saturn V burns the last of its fuel and falls away. The loss of thrust hurls the astronauts forward. Luckily, they are held in place by their straps. Moments later the second stage erupts, burning its fuel and slamming the astronauts back into their seats by the force of the acceleration. When the second stage separates from the command and service modules, the men are thrust forward again. Once out of Earth's gravity, they are weightless.

The Saturn V Launch Vehicle

The Saturn V launch vehicle, used in the Apollo 11 space mission, had three stages, or sections, each with its own powerful engines and fuel. The stages fell away from the spacecraft when their fuel had been used up. They burned up as they fell back to Earth through the atmosphere.

1. Launches and orbits Earth

2. Orbits and lands on the moon

3. Takes off from the moon

4. Returns back home

Now it is time for Michael Collins to separate the command module *Columbia* and its service module from the third stage of Saturn, turn around, and connect with the lunar module *Eagle,* stored in the remaining section of the Saturn V. The lunar module is the vehicle that will land on the moon. Unless the two spacecraft are docked correctly, Aldrin and Armstrong will not be able to enter the lunar landing module.

Everything goes perfectly. *Columbia*'s nose makes a clean connection to the top of the *Eagle*. It heads for the moon, and Saturn's third stage moves slowly away. At this point the three astronauts have been working for fourteen hours straight since the time of liftoff. They've earned a rest and go to sleep at 10:30 P.M.

July 17

About 9 A.M., the crew eats breakfast. There is no newspaper delivery in space, so Mission Control gives them a summary of the day's news, including sports! They successfully test the engine that will carry them into lunar orbit so they can land on the moon.

Shortly after 7:30 P.M., they begin a thirty-six minute color TV broadcast from the spacecraft. Viewers on Earth can see the inside of the command module.

July 18

Mission Control lets the astronauts sleep an extra hour. After breakfast, they check fuel levels, charge batteries, and dump waste water into space. They give another TV broadcast later in the day, talking to the people back home for over an hour and a half. As viewers watch, the **hatch** to the lunar module is opened. Commander Armstrong, followed by Buzz Aldrin, squeezes through the small tunnel to inspect the *Eagle*.

Buzz Aldrin

7

The moon as seen from Apollo 11

July 19

The astronauts wake up early but are told they can sleep for another hour and a half. After breakfast, housekeeping chores, and the daily news report, the astronauts see the moon. They have not been able to see it for almost a whole day. It now appears much larger and closer through the window of *Columbia,* a sight no one on Earth has ever been able to see.

Soon the astronauts pass around the moon. They are ready for the first engine burn. The burst slams the men back in their seats. This burn ends after six minutes. A second burn will place them in an orbit closer to the moon. Then Armstrong and Aldrin will prepare to separate from the *Columbia* and land on the moon's surface in the *Eagle.* These burns must be perfect. Luckily, because of great care and practice, both burns go very well.

A little before 4 P.M., they begin a thirty-five minute telecast of the moon's surface. The camera shows the area chosen as the *Eagle*'s landing site. Armstrong and Aldrin test the *Eagle* once again. They set out all the clothing and equipment they will need for their walk on the moon tomorrow.

This photo of Earth rising over the lunar **horizon** is one of the most famous photos taken during any space flight. As the astronauts look at planet Earth from space, what thoughts do they have? Do they wonder how all three of them got to this shared place in history?

Earth rising over the lunar horizon

The Apollo 11 Crew

From left to right: Commander Neil A. Armstrong, command module pilot Michael Collins, lunar module pilot Edwin E. "Buzz" Aldrin, Jr.

Neil Armstrong

Neil A. Armstrong was born on his grandparents' farm in Ohio. He fell in love with flying after he saw an Ohio air show with his father. He was inspired to fly at seven years old after he took his first airplane ride in the "Tin Goose," one of the first all-metal planes to carry passengers.

As Neil grew older, his love of flying also grew. He built model airplanes and made a wind tunnel in the family basement to test them. He read every book on flying he could find. At age fifteen, he started working to make enough money for flying lessons. He earned his pilot's license just one year later, at sixteen.

During the Korean War, Armstrong flew fighter jets. His seventy-eight combat missions earned him three medals. He later completed college degrees in aeronautical engineering and aerospace engineering. As a NASA pilot, he tested the F-102 supersonic fighter and the X-15 rocket plane.

Neil Armstrong was selected as an astronaut in 1962. Four years later, he commanded space flight Gemini 8. Each step of his career inched him closer to his role as commander of Apollo 11 and one of the two men who would land and walk on the moon.

Neil Armstrong

Edwin "Buzz"
Aldrin at age 3

Edwin "Buzz" Aldrin

Edwin Aldrin was born in Montclair, New Jersey, on January 20, 1930. He played in the park, learned to pole vault, and loved football. Aldrin went to West Point after high school and, like Armstrong, flew combat missions in Korea.

Aldrin was turned down the first time he applied for the astronaut program, but he didn't give up. In 1963, after earning an advanced degree in astronautics, Aldrin was accepted as a NASA astronaut. He found the space program very different from flying combat missions in Korea. In combat, Aldrin explained, you have to make snap decisions and constantly respond quickly to the unknown. In space, it is very different. You learn to make slow, carefully thought-out decisions and try hard to avoid making mistakes. He was perfectly suited to his job on Apollo 11. He piloted the lunar module that carried him and Neil Armstrong to the moon and back again. He also walked on the moon.

Michael Collins

Michael Collins

Michael Collins was born in Rome, Italy, on October 31, 1930. He later moved to Washington, D.C. Collins had much in common with Armstrong and Aldrin. He also chose flying as a career. After graduating from West Point, he tested jet fighters for the Air Force. Collins spent a lot of time in the sky, logging over four thousand hours of flying time.

Collins was named a NASA astronaut in 1963. He was the backup pilot for the Gemini 7 mission and a pilot on the Gemini 10 mission, in which he docked with another spacecraft. During Apollo 11, Michael Collins's job was to command the *Columbia* and continue to orbit the moon while Armstrong and Aldrin descended to the lunar surface in the *Eagle*, and then successfully dock with the lunar module and return home.

Just as the backgrounds of his fellow astronauts helped pave their way to the moon, Collins's life experiences helped him. As pilot on Apollo 11, Collins succeeded with flying colors.

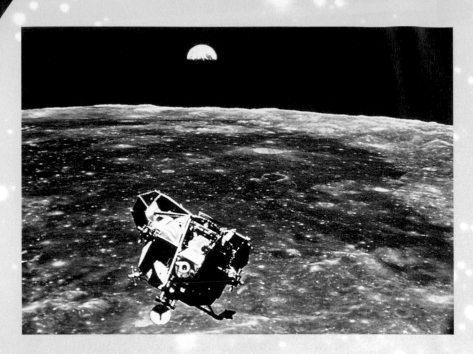

"The *Eagle* Has Landed!"

On July 20, 1969, just four days after liftoff, Armstrong and Aldrin open the hatch between *Columbia* and *Eagle*. They float into the craft and prepare it for its flight to the lunar surface. Everything looks good. Later that day, the lunar module *Eagle* is ready to separate from the *Columbia*.

Armstrong and Aldrin slowly separate from the command module and, strapped in a standing position, begin their slow descent to the lunar surface.

The lunar module *Eagle* has four legs dangling awkwardly in all directions from its body. On the *Eagle* with the astronauts are some scientific instruments that they will place on the moon's surface.

The men are six thousand feet above the surface when a yellow caution light flickers to life. Luckily, Mission Control assures them there is nothing to worry about. At 4:18 P.M., the *Eagle* lands at the Sea of Tranquility, an area of the moon filled not with water but with dark solidified lava. Armstrong reports the welcome news to Mission Control: "Houston, Tranquility base here—the *Eagle* has landed."

Houston later finds out that Armstrong's quick decisions saved the *Eagle* as he took control and piloted it to a safe landing location, avoiding a field of boulders and a large crater. After landing, they had less than thirty seconds of fuel left.

The *Eagle* is now separated from the *Columbia*.

"One Giant Leap for Mankind"

The two men are supposed to rest after landing, but they are too excited to sleep. They decide to walk on the moon earlier than planned.

It still takes hours to get ready. In fact, it takes them over two hours just to get their 180-pound spacesuits on, even without the pull of Earth's gravity. A little over six hours after landing, Neil Armstrong slowly squeezes through the hatch. He has a life support and communication system strapped to his shoulders. He moves slowly down the nine steps of the ladder, stopping on the last step before putting his left foot on the lunar surface. He is now the first human to walk on the moon. As he takes his first step, millions of people watching back on Earth hear him speak these now famous words:

"That's one small step for man, one giant leap for mankind."

Aldrin backs out of the spacecraft onto the lunar surface, and the two men spend the next few hours collecting moon rocks, drilling core samples, and taking photographs. They test ways of moving around, including kangaroo hops on two feet. They figure out that an easy run is the best way to move.

Armstrong and Aldrin plant the U.S. flag on the soil and take a phone call from President Richard Nixon. The men also leave a plaque on the moon. The plaque reads:

> HERE MEN FROM THE PLANET EARTH
> FIRST SET FOOT UPON THE MOON
> JULY 1969 A.D.
> WE CAME IN PEACE FOR ALL MANKIND

Because there is no wind or water to wear away the moon's surface, the footprints left by the astronauts in the Sea of Tranquility will probably last for millions of years.

The Spacesuit

In earlier space flights, men walked in space with a tether that attached their spacesuit to the spacecraft. For Apollo 11, the suit design needed to change to both protect the astronauts and give them freedom to bend, lift, and walk on the rough ground. Each of the nine parts of these suits was designed for a specific purpose.

Life support–controls the oxygen, pressure, ventilation, and communication

Emergency oxygen–provides backup in case the main life support unit fails

Helmet–anchored to the suit, but astronauts can turn their heads side to side inside the helmet

Visors–protect the astronauts' eyes from ultraviolet radiation and seal oxygen inside

Gloves–made from casts of the astronauts' hands to increase flexibility

Joints–molded rubber joints added at bending parts of the body make it possible for the astronauts to move and walk freely to conduct experiments

Layered suit–several layers to protect, insulate, and ventilate their bodies

Neck ring–attaches the helmet to the space suit

Boots–include an overshoe designed to fit over the spacesuit boot

Emergency oxygen

Helmet

Visors

Neck ring

Gloves

Life support

Joints

Layered suit

Boots

19

Armstrong and Aldrin spend less than one Earth day on the moon's surface. The actual moonwalk lasts just two and one-half hours, yet it changes everything. The dream of touching the moon has become a reality.

The astronauts return to the lunar module and get some sleep. About seven hours later Mission Control awakens them. It's time to redock with the *Columbia*.

Back in the *Columbia*, Michael Collins is nervous. What if the *Eagle*'s engine won't start? What if the docking doesn't happen and something goes wrong? He does not want to think about returning to Earth without his fellow travelers. But he does not have to worry. Shortly before 2:00 P.M. on July 21, the *Eagle*'s engine fires, lifting Armstrong and Aldrin off the lunar surface. *Eagle* successfully redocks with the *Columbia*. Aldrin and Armstrong join Collins. The *Eagle*'s job is done. It won't return to Earth with the *Columbia*. It will drift off as planned, remaining in lunar orbit to this day.

Apollo 11 splashes down in the Pacific Ocean on July 24, 1969. The astronauts spend three weeks in **quarantine,** or isolation, while scientists make sure that they have not brought back any germs from the moon. They can finally greet their families and the world in August.

Apollo 11 splashes down into the Pacific Ocean.

The Apollo 11 crew speaks to President Richard Nixon while in quarantine.

The astronauts are honored with a parade in New York.

Since Apollo 11

After Apollo 11, Neil Armstrong worked at NASA and taught engineering. He also served on the Presidential Commission that investigated the explosion of the *Challenger* spacecraft.

After Apollo 11, Buzz Aldrin returned to the Air Force and then retired a year later. He worked with NASA's Lunar-Mars Exploration Office. He has written books about space, including *Return to Earth,* about the flight of Apollo 11, and a science-fiction book, *Encounter with Tiber.* He also developed a plan for connecting Mars and Earth by using a constantly moving spacecraft.

After leaving NASA in 1970, Michael Collins ran the National Air and Space Museum in Washington, D.C., for several years. He has written *Carrying the Fire* and *Flying to the Moon and other Strange Places.*

Apollo 11 was a huge step. Each generation must continue to move forward, rise to challenges, and achieve its goals. In your time, what do you think that next giant step will be?

People visit the Apollo 11 command module inside the Air and Space Museum in Washington, D.C.

Glossary

astronauts *n.* members of the crew of a spacecraft.

capsule *n.* the enclosed front section of a rocket made to carry instruments, astronauts, etc., into space.

hatch *n.* a trapdoor covering an opening in an aircraft's or ship's deck; hatchway cover.

horizon *n.* the line where land and sky seem to meet; skyline.

lunar *adj.* of, like, or about the moon.

module *n.* a self-contained unit or system within a larger system, often designed for a particular function.

quarantine *n.* detention, isolation, and other measures taken to prevent the spread of an infectious disease.